MW01222693

A Man A Fish

Also by Donna-Michelle St. Bernard:
Gas Girls
Salome's Clothes (included in the anthology *Performing Back*, edited by Dalbir Singh)

A Man A Fish

Donna-Michelle St. Bernard

Playwrights Canada Press
Toronto

A Man A Fish © 2015 by Donna-Michelle St. Bernard

No part of this book may be reproduced, downloaded, or used in any form
or by any means without the prior written permission of the publisher,
except for excerpts in a review or by a licence from Access Copyright,
www.accesscopyright.ca.

For professional or amateur production rights, please contact:
Michael Petrasek at The Talent House
204A St. George Street, Toronto, ON M5R 2N5
416.960.9686, michael@talenthouse.ca

Library and Archives Canada Cataloguing in Publication
St. Bernard, Donna-Michelle, author
        A man a fish / Donna-Michelle St. Bernard.

A play.
Issued in print and electronic formats.
ISBN 978-1-77091-434-6 (paperback).--ISBN 978-1-77091-435-3 (pdf).--
ISBN 978-1-77091-436-0 (html).--ISBN 978-1-77091-437-7 (mobi)

        I. Title.

PS8637.A4525M35 2015   C812'.6   C2015-904075-2
                                                C2015-904076-0

We acknowledge the financial support of the Canada Council for the Arts, the
Ontario Arts Council (OAC), the Ontario Media Development Corporation,
and the Government of Canada through the Canada Book Fund for our
publishing activities. Nous remercions l'appui financier du Conseil des Arts du
Canada, le Conseil des arts de l'Ontario (CAO), la Société de développement
de l'industrie des médias de l'Ontario, et le Gouvernement du Canada par
l'entremise du Fonds du livre du Canada pour nos activités d'édition.

For Angela Rebeiro, who told me exactly how it was going to be.
For Kern and Mom.
Also, God.

Introduction
by Jivesh Parasram

Often when I read a play my mind jumps forward into staging, lighting, the possibility of working in slapstick . . . Generally speaking, the written word itself becomes less important than what the play evokes in my mind. However, this is not the case with Donna-Michelle St. Bernard's work. I have to stop and listen to the sound these words make, and imagine the rhythm that they could pulse when woven together and brought to life. The script is a score. I've known DM for a relatively short time; however, in that time I have, without fail, been ceaselessly impressed and halted by the power of her writing. This play, which you are about to read, is no exception.

A play like this carries a certain richness that is rare to find. DM has a way of being able to create the most heart-wrenching, honest, and poetic scenarios—and then gleefully sabotage these moments with a single comedic jab to make the tears you just wept get snorted back up in an undignified laugh. For me, that's what the purpose of theatre really is. Perhaps more than many other art forms, theatre allows us to stretch our vulnerabilities out and shake them dry with humour. But only if the playwright is brave enough to *not* take their artistry to be prophetic "feelyness"—which is not a word—but then again, neither is ginormous. And now both of them are published.

Silliness aside, I do mean to identify this, the almost musical ability to use a spectrum of emotion, to be one of the great strengths of DM's ability as a playwright. And it is no accident. I once received a new draft of a play from DM—it was actually about three drafts further along than when I had read it last. Reading it again I knew something was different; it felt different. And yet I couldn't put my finger on what, exactly, had changed. When I went back to the older draft for comparison I found minute changes that I would have missed altogether if the actual weight of the piece hadn't shifted so considerably.

Everything matters. And everything is well thought out. It's this craft and dedication that allows the playwright to take a very real topic—such as, say . . . the current practices of neo-colonial fisheries—and show you the human story around this issue. But that would just be a *good* playwright; what makes this playwright *exceptional* is that, if you pay very close attention, you can see that this human story itself is a web of parallels, metaphors, and landscapes; so complex a web that the only way to make sense of it is to step back and take it all in. If there's one thing that sums up for me the experience of engaging with DM's work—it very much is to enjoy the silence, because there is never a moment that the silence isn't part of the full composition.

But praise aside now. In this play I would ask you to consider a few images and ideas: Ripples, the circular vibrations formed from one impact point reverberating ad infinitum. Clinks and clanks, the sound of tin on tin, or of any substance really when clashing with its own kin. Horizons, the points at which the terrestrial disappears or kisses its opposite, points that challenge our notions of fully perceiving time. And finally, running. What exactly do we run from, what do we run to, and what stops us?

Of course, there's more. There's always so much more. So go, bask in some beauty, and meet sadness with a grin.

Jivesh Parasram is a multidisciplinary artist, facilitator, and researcher. His past artistic work has explored themes of human security, migrant populations, and international law. His current work deals with affect, disidentification, and the critical aesthetics of resistance. He is a founding member of Pandemic Theatre (www.pandemictheatre.ca), a Toronto-based theatre collective that creates, develops, and produces socio-political work from critical and marginalized perspectives.

A Man A Fish was first produced by Persephone Theatre at the Backstage Stage in Saskatoon, Saskatchewan, between October 23 and November 3, 2013, and featured the following cast and creative team:

Prosper: Peter N. Bailey
Solange: Nicole Joy-Fraser
Eddy: Johnny Trinh
Edige: Matt Burgess

Director: Philip Adams
Assistant director: Lauren Holfeuer
Dramaturge: Philip Adams
Publication dramaturge: Sarah Garton Stanley
Set design: Jenna Maren
Sound design and music composition: Gilles Zloty
Lighting design: David Granger
Costume design: Jeff Chief
Stage management: Dustyn Wales

Characters

Prosper: fisherman
Solange: fishwife
Eddy: eel salesman
Edige: bartender
Ines: possibly a ghost, or an imagining, or a diversion. In any case . . .

Settings

House: Home of Prosper and Solange. Mostly the kitchen and bedroom.
Bar: Bar operated by Edige. Can be indoor, or a roadside kiosk.
Lake: Prosper's fishing spot on the bank of a ginormous lake.
Room: Eddy's rented room. Stifling. May be unseen or only a window.

Notes On Text

A backslash (\) indicates the character is actively not responding.

1. All I Need Is

Movement One: SOLANGE *kisses* PROSPER *goodbye as he leaves their house. He sits at the lake, fishing line in the water. After a while he hears something on the opposite shore, smiles, watches. He returns home and is greeted by* SOLANGE, *who takes the fish from his full line.* PROSPER *goes to the bar. A buyer passes and takes the fish from* SOLANGE; *she puts money in a wish jar and then kisses the jar.*

SOLANGE: Good morning, little one! Did you pass the night well? Look. Look at how the sun sits just in the top of that tree as though in a nest, resting before it completes its climb to noonday, when your father will turn towards home again. The sun sees us admiring him, but instead of coming closer he moves further away, afraid that we might see his flaws. That is what the sun is like.

Your father can't wait to meet you, believe me. There are just a few more things to make ready before we can hope to welcome you into the warmth of my blood and flesh. Oh, have I shown you this? Look here, between the paving stones. Do you see the tiny white flower that has struggled to exist? It is a flower that some will call a weed simply because it does not ask our efforts to grow. They did not tell it to be there, and for that reason they would pull it out by the root.

EDDY *arrives and stands outside the bar with his suitcase.*

SOLANGE *passes on the other side of the bar.* EDIGE *hears her passing and goes to the window.*

EDIGE: Good morning, good woman.

SOLANGE *ignores him and continues on.* EDIGE *smiles as though she has responded.*

Mn. Good God.

2. A Good, Quiet Spot

Just outside the door of the house. PROSPER *is exiting defensively.*

SOLANGE: Prosper! Prosper, wait. What do you mean it feels small? It's the same house we went to sleep in last night. Did you grow while you slept?

PROSPER: I don't know, it just feels too small right now. I'm going fishing.

SOLANGE: What a surprise.

PROSPER: Of course it's not a surprise, Solange. I don't get up every morning just to get away from you. I have to work. No fish, no money, right?

SOLANGE: Make sure you don't fall into any holes.

PROSPER: What?

SOLANGE: What about your pole?

She hands it to him.

PROSPER: Thanks.

SOLANGE: Mm hm. And make sure it's only fish you're catching, hey?

PROSPER: \

> PROSPER *leaves without kissing her; he sits beside a ginormous lake, pole in the water.* EDDY *shows up.*

EDDY: Say there, friend. Helluva day. Good fishing here?

PROSPER: Nope.

EDDY: Catch any fish today?

PROSPER: Nope.

EDDY: Yesterday?

PROSPER: No.

EDDY: Ah, a bad spot. A never catch nothing spot. A hide from wife spot.

PROSPER: No.

EDDY: *(clarifying)* But it's not a good spot.

> PROSPER *clears his throat.*

You're not exactly verbose, are you? No, that's all right. I can take a hint. Always been perceptive. I was standing over there just now, seen you over here and I said to myself, there's a man ain't caught no fish. There's a man, something on his mind. There's a smart man, I said to myself, and you know what else? Yessir. A man who can recognize an opportunity when he sees one.

PROSPER: \

EDDY: Doesn't even need to get excited about it, just takes it as it comes. Yes.

PROSPER: \

EDDY: Not too much of a talker myself, you know.

PROSPER: You forget your rod?

EDDY: No, not fishing today. Just kind of checking out the waters.

PROSPER: Hm.

EDDY: Sorry, what's that?

　　　PROSPER *coughs, scratches.*

So, friend, you got any tips on good fishing spots around here?

PROSPER: You should go over there.

EDDY: Over by that tree?

PROSPER: Sure.

EDDY: Or maybe there, behind that rock?

PROSPER: Okay.

EDDY: So, the rock then, or the tree?

PROSPER: Yeah.

EDDY: Thanks. I gotta tell you, I sure appreciate the advice, friend. It's rough being new in town, you know? And it's just good of you to reach out like that. Sure hope to repay the favour some day. Hope you don't mind, I'm just gonna head on over there . . . or there. Thanks again!

3. Windy

PROSPER is drinking at the bar.

PROSPER: It's not a matter of reluctance; it's a matter of stability. You don't build a house in shifting swamplands. You don't plant seed in rocky ground. You don't crack an egg over a cold stove. You prepare, man. You prepare. And then you act. For example, I wouldn't ask you to begin pouring before holding out this empty glass, would I? Makes no sense.

> *PROSPER holds out his empty glass suggestively, then taps it twice on the counter to underscore his request. EDIGE fills it.*

EDIGE: Taking your time tonight, Prosper.

PROSPER: Just a short pause in the journey, Edige.

EDIGE: Been two or three pauses now.

PROSPER: You trying to get rid of me?

EDIGE: Just trying to keep you on the warm side of the bed.

PROSPER: If I thought a warm bed was waiting I would already be gone. Anyways. Dinner time. Last one.

> PROSPER *puts money on the counter, slams the drink back, and goes home to find* SOLANGE *waiting, agitated.*

Solange, I'm home.

SOLANGE: Now you come home? Now? Why did you wait until now?

PROSPER: Solange, what's the matter?

SOLANGE: Oh, husband, have mercy and kill me now so that I can be spared this humiliation. Is it for this that I left my father's house, following a trail of sweet words to end sitting here in silence? Have I left behind my mother and sisters to be set upon by every manner of indignity in my own home?

PROSPER: What is it now?

SOLANGE: Look! Look at this! Do you see what she does now? Look at how my pot is sticky and my kitchen smells of burning corn. Ah, I know her game. I grind, measure, boil, as I have done a hundred times before. I add meal to the water and as I turn my back to get salt she blows on the fire, making it blaze up, and this burning smell seeps through the town carrying about the news of my wasteful stupidity and makes it easy to believe that I am a bad wife. Surely the elders will let you quit me if this continues. Oh, you greedy woman. You want all of him? Should I grow old alone with nothing to keep me but the pity of other forgotten old women? Or would you like me to leave this house and walk west until someone takes me?

PROSPER: I don't even know what to say to you right now.

SOLANGE: You know what to say to her. I hear you whispering at night. I don't know what you're saying, but I know who you're saying it to. Why is she here? Don't her people keep a shrine?

PROSPER: Solange.

SOLANGE: Yes, Prosper? . . .

PROSPER: I'm not hungry.

> PROSPER *tries to touch the ceiling with his fingertips. He sits outside a while, then goes behind the house and takes some measurements with his eyes.*

One day I will come home and say, Solange, my basket is full for you. You will tell me it is more than we need, with your open arms waiting to welcome me, with your open mouth smiling contentedly, with no sharp corners on your lips or your eyes.

4. Communing

Simultaneously we see SOLANGE *in her house making ritual,* PROSPER *at the lake fishing,* EDIGE *in the bar pining/moon-gazing, and* EDDY *smoking on his back in bed.*

SOLANGE *lays down a handful of seeds, a small branch, and some leaves in a bowl and lights them, then lays the bowl under the bed.*

SOLANGE: Ines. Tonight we will talk, you and I.

I see women just like you every day at the clinic. Women from over the mountain who would not so closely shame their families; women who will travel a distance with a little piece of home in your hand, all this way to take our men . . . and, eventually, to see our doctors. You felt strong then because my husband wanted you, but his life is with me, and yours is ended now.

You know, I didn't mind when you were alive, standing under that fig tree where he could not fail to see you. As long as he paid you, it was only a business transaction. Money in exchange for physical needs. Sowing of seeds in arid soil. Now . . . Why don't you leave? What can he give you now? You should move on. Go to your family where you can do some good. I am for his real needs.

I see women like me every day, too. A plot tilled and ready for planting, left untended while a crow eats the seeds before they can root. Feeling something out of place in their marriage bed. Knowing where it came from but not saying. Faithful husbands.

She lies down in the bed.

I hope I dream that you have decided to leave him.

Inside the bar after closing.

EDIGE: Solange, my beloved, I came too late to win your love, but I would move a mountain if only to catch your eye. To make you happy I would tear down the sky and feed it into the lake that you might bathe among clouds as angels do. Solange, I would gladly break my spine to build the spires of your temple. I would cut short the number of my days to extend yours. I would split my skull to show you how earnest are my dreams of your joy.

EDIGE lies down behind the bar to sleep. PROSPER is seen at the lake, rod against a tree, listening to memory stones echo.

5. Here to Help

PROSPER is drinking at the bar.

PROSPER: Bartender, another dozen.

EDIGE: You need a dozen lashes to your backside.

PROSPER: Indeed I do.

EDIGE: And I would gladly give them to you, but it makes your woman sad to see you suffer.

PROSPER: Better make 'em drinks, then.

PROSPER does calculations throughout on a worn notepad with a stub of pencil.

EDDY: *(seeing PROSPER)* There you are.

EDIGE: There he is. Same time, every damned day.

PROSPER: Just trying to put bread in your mouth.

EDIGE: You're a prince.

Turns to EDDY.

And what can I wet you with?

EDDY: Whaddaya got?

EDIGE: Choice and free will, same as you.

EDDY: I wouldn't say no to a whiskey.

EDIGE: Here you go.

EDDY *drinks.*

EDDY: Gawd. That's not whiskey, it's—what is that?

EDIGE: Chibuku.

EDDY: What happened to choice?

EDIGE: Round here it is every man's choice to call it what they want, but is only chibuku we serve.

EDDY: Ugh.

EDIGE: What brings you this way?

EDDY: I am here to make things better.

EDIGE: Eh! What do you know. We're in the same business. Right now I am helping Prosper to make things better in his spirit.

EDDY: What do you know indeed! This is the very same man I am here to help!

PROSPER: All this help and nobody asking what the problem is.

EDIGE: What brand of poison you peddle?

EDDY: Progress.

EDIGE: Better if it was peanuts, but I guess that's fine. Myself, I offer tonic for all manner of joylessness, pain, and solitude.

EDDY: And which does our friend suffer from?

EDIGE: One of each at least. His girlfriend is dead and his wife is still living, crying for a child he will not give her.

EDDY: Woman trouble. Make his next drink on me.

EDIGE: Look, I don't mind you putting out your bait here but if you want to stick around to reel it in it's gonna cost you. Have a drink. Nobody trust a man in a bar too good to drink.

EDIGE pours a drink. EDDY drinks, chokes.

EDDY: It's good.

6. A Gift Horse

PROSPER *sits beside a ginormous lake, fishing.* EDDY *sits down with a six-pack of beer. He opens one and hands one to* PROSPER. *They drink together.*

EDDY: You were right. Fishing's way better over there. Almost perfect, some would say.

PROSPER: I told you.

EDDY: So why do you keep fishing here?

PROSPER: Used to be quieter.

EDDY: Like the quiet, huh? You got a wife? Kids?

PROSPER: Wife. No children.

EDDY: Wife's enough.

PROSPER: Believe me.

EDDY: Thing with women is, there's never enough, right?

PROSPER: That's right.

EDDY: Always wanna know where it came from and where it went.

PROSPER: And so suspicious.

EDDY: Oh?

PROSPER: It's ridiculous.

EDDY: You don't say.

PROSPER: Where you going? When you coming back?

EDDY: Sounds like she thinks you have a girlfriend.

PROSPER: Everyone knows I had a girlfriend. That's not the point.

EDDY: Listen, I'm not one to give advice, but let me tell you something. The answer to your problem with your wife is this: more. Just give her more. Something. Anything. That's what they want.

PROSPER: I don't have any more. This is what I have.

EDDY: But what if you could get more.

PROSPER: What if.

EDDY: What if.

PROSPER: What if.

EDDY: \

PROSPER: \

EDDY: Good lake you got here.

PROSPER: Yes. This lake is like a mother who gives forth endlessly whatever feeds us, body and soul, so that we are strong enough to live, to thrive, to dream. It's a good lake.

EDDY: These fish in this lake. They're all right.

PROSPER: They're good.

EDDY: But wouldn't it be good if this lake also had eel?

PROSPER: Hm, I don't know. The lake has plenty of fish.

EDDY: But it could also have eel.

PROSPER: Mm, it's pretty good the way it is.

EDDY: Actually, you only feel that way because you've never caught an eel. No one has around here. Do you know how much people at the market will pay you for this eel?

PROSPER: Probably quite a lot.

EDDY: You see where I'm going with this.

PROSPER: Mm, I still like this lake quite a lot. It's got that tree over there, that rock, all those fish, and way on the other side . . .

EDDY: Listen to me, Prosper. I am trying to say that I've got an eel that will seed your fortune after only three months of growth. This is the goose that lays the golden egg. These are the beans that grew the beanstalk. And I can get many more! Stock your lake and make you rich. Because you're a friend, I will sell you this eel for only a small sum, and you can see for yourself. You will definitely want more.

PROSPER: No, thanks. I don't think I want any eels.

EDDY: Well, think it over.

PROSPER: I'll do that.

EDDY: \

PROSPER: Oh, you mean now.

EDDY: Yeah.

PROSPER: Okay.

EDDY: \

PROSPER: \

EDDY: You're not really thinking about it.

PROSPER: No.

EDDY: Well, listen. This is what I'm going to do. Since I did bring this eel all the way up here I'm going to go ahead and release it here in the lake. Because you're a friend, and you helped me out before.

PROSPER: There's really no need—

EDDY: I insist.

    EDDY *throws the eel into the lake.*

PROSPER: What the—?

EDDY: So, hey, I'll see you at the bar later, right? Right on.

PROSPER: What do you even do?

EDDY: I'm doing it now.

PROSPER: And that's good for you?

EDDY: Working out so far.

    EDDY exits.

7. Receipts

The bar.

EDDY: A year ago I could have been in and out of here in three days. But now, with the Fisheries Department behind the project, it's all about service. What I'm trying to say is—what the hell is that noise?

PROSPER: Receipts.

EDDY: Right . . .

PROSPER: Edige. He counts receipts the whole shift. Always got his hand on a franc, this one.

EDDY: If you don't want to tell me—

PROSPER: Wait.

   PROSPER *drains his glass.*

Edige, another.

   Having anticipated this, EDIGE *is opening one at his elbow.*

EDIGE: Already there.

PROSPER: My man.

EDDY: Very good. You ordered a drink.

> EDIGE *adds the new bottle cap to a pile in his pocket and*
> *jangles it.*

PROSPER: Yes, but you hear that sound? Means I haven't paid for it.

EDDY: Is he gonna do that all night?

PROSPER: Only till I pay him.

EDDY: Then pay him already.

PROSPER: Oh, you get used to it. Lucky thing is, the louder the noise
gets, the drunker I am, so I just don't care.

EDDY: But the money's in your pocket.

PROSPER: Yup.

EDDY: Just give it to him.

PROSPER: Nope. Money's in my pocket. For at least another hour I
have money. I like that feeling.

EDDY: Don't you want it to stop? It's so irritating.

PROSPER: Don't care. Drunk.

EDDY: Well I'm not.

PROSPER: Sorry for you.

EDDY: Pay him.

PROSPER: Nope.

EDDY: Dammit. Barkeep, what's he owe? Here. Take it. Gawd. You listen to that all night, every night?

PROSPER: No. Sometimes some irritable asshole from Fisheries comes along and pays my tab.

EDDY: Well.

    Beat.

Fair enough.

    EDDY takes a swig, grimaces, slides it away. EDIGE carefully returns the remnants to a bottle and re-caps it securely.

8. Communing—Pressure

Inside the house. PROSPER *enters, wipes down his pole, and sits.* SOLANGE *tentatively rubs his back.*

SOLANGE: You are at the lake often, even after the sun is high. I am alone here longer each day, feeding my thoughts downstream, hoping they will snag your line.

SOLANGE lies down. PROSPER *sits against the wall.*

PROSPER: That lake is like a coffer that has been filled with little treasures for me to seek out and cherish.

SOLANGE: So is my heart.

PROSPER: I am so tired.

SOLANGE: Husband, come over here and lie beside me.

PROSPER: That bed makes me feel like I'm rolling down a hill. It's not big enough.

PROSPER goes to SOLANGE and lies uncomfortably with her.

SOLANGE: I can smell your fishing rod from here.

PROSPER: I cleaned it.

SOLANGE: Well it smells funny. Different.

PROSPER: Sorry.

SOLANGE: Well?

> PROSPER *exhales loudly, gets out of bed.*

Where are you going in the middle of the night?

> PROSPER *leans the rod against the wall outside the door and gets back in bed. It is quiet for a moment.*

The shape of your hand is different. You touch my body like this. See? Cupping your hand to hold a belly that does not hang there. You touch me like this. See? And there is a whole field of space in here where we are apart. You are not touching me at all. Open your eyes. Make your hand in the shape of my body. Like this.

PROSPER: Give me peace.

SOLANGE: What?

PROSPER: Go to sleep, Solange.

SOLANGE: Each time that you roll over in your sleep beside me I know that her hand is stroking you. You smile in your sleep lately. Your mouth turns up until your teeth show and I know you are nibbling at her flesh like the little fish at your knees in the shallows. Sleep in the yard tonight. See if that woman will lower herself to the dirt for you.

> PROSPER *leaves. We see* SOLANGE *in her house making ritual,* PROSPER *at the lake fishing, and* EDIGE *in the bar pining.*

EDIGE: Solange, I recall the smoothness of your brow before he creased it, the fullness of your smile before he turned it, the maybe of your love before he claimed it. I am too old, now, to learn another lure.

EDIGE lies down behind the bar to sleep.

SOLANGE lays down a handful of seeds, a small branch, and some leaves in a bowl and lights them, then lays the bowl under the bed.

SOLANGE: Ines. I recall the smoothness of your skin before sickness took you. You have to believe that I never wished your illness. I never hoped harm for you, only that Prosper would always come home to me when he left you. You never replaced me, only filled a need I was not shaped for. But now is the time for you to rest. I will take care of him now.

SOLANGE lies in bed and sees the empty space on the shelf. PROSPER is seen at the lake, rod against a tree, listening to memory stones echo.

PROSPER: Little one, do you see how the moon lies there in the water, cooling her feet before carrying on? The sun has chased her all day without hope of even a glimpse, and she laughs and splashes, unconcerned with his exhaustion. That is what the moon is like.

What peace you will bring your mother when you come. Just wait a little longer while I make ready.

9. Baiting

PROSPER *is pacing by the lake when* EDDY *approaches jauntily.*

EDDY: Ho there, friend. How's the wife?

PROSPER: Hey, uh—

EDDY: Eddy. Eddy by name, eddy by nature.

PROSPER: Eddy. What is this green stuff all over the place? This lake is like a stew gone cold, growing a skin across its surface that will soon congeal its depths. Look, you have to fix this. That eel you released in my lake is eating all the fish, and I can't catch it. What's the deal?

EDDY: Oh! My friend, did I not tell you about the bait that you need to catch the eel?

PROSPER: No you didn't, and I swear I've tried everything I know from all my many years of fishing in this lake. Well, don't just stand there. Tell me. What kind of bait will catch this eel? I have to get it out of my lake while there are still fish left.

EDDY: Not to worry, friend. I can sell you some bait for that eel for only a small sum—almost at cost. Because you are a friend of mine.

PROSPER: Never mind the friend stuff. How much do you want for it?

EDDY: Fourteen thousand francs.

PROSPER: I don't happen to have that on me.

EDDY: That's all right. I'll come for it later.

PROSPER: No, thank you.

EDDY: Cool, cool. I guess you can just leave that eel in there, see how it plays out . . .

PROSPER: I'll buy your bait and it will be the last piece of business we do.

EDDY: Oh, don't be like that. Happy fishing.

PROSPER: Why aren't you gone yet?

EDDY holds out a business card.

EDDY: I just want you to know that if you happen to want me, for any reason, you can reach me—

PROSPER: I won't be wanting you.

EDDY: Oh I think you will.

EDDY tosses down the card.

10. Too Close

Movement Two: SOLANGE *kisses* PROSPER *goodbye as he distractedly leaves his house. He sits at the lake, fishing line in the water, but looking at the opposite shore. A stone is heard falling into the water in memory.* PROSPER *smiles. He looks down by his feet and sees a single bright stone that he takes. After a while he leaves the lake, returns home.* SOLANGE *comes out and notes the time, then the half-empty line.* PROSPER *puts the stone in the garden and goes to the bar. A buyer passes and takes the fish from* SOLANGE; *the money is too little, so she removes a picture of a fish from the wall and sells that too. She puts money in the wish jar.*

EDDY *approaches the house.* SOLANGE *emerges shaking out a rag mat.*

EDDY: Good morning! This is nice. A very nice place to lay down one's head.

SOLANGE: Hm.

EDDY: And a lovely head to lay it next to.

SOLANGE: Hmph.

EDDY: That bartender was absolutely right about you.

SOLANGE: Are you looking for my husband?

EDDY: If I am, then I'm looking for one lucky man.

SOLANGE: You can tell him that when you find him. I don't know where he is.

SOLANGE starts back inside.

EDDY: What's this say?

SOLANGE: Can't you read it?

EDDY: Kind of.

SOLANGE: It looks perfectly clear to me.

EDDY: Unite . . . Travail . . . Proper?

SOLANGE: Prosper. Obviously.

EDDY: Yes, of course. That's very nice. Three very nice little ideas.

SOLANGE: Prosper made it, when we first moved in. He saw the words on a sign in town. It suits him.

EDDY: I suppose it does. It's . . . homey.

SOLANGE: Homey.

EDDY: It has . . . quaint charm. Of course they do say opposites attract. This kind of sign suits this kind of house, suits that kind of man. But you, I can see you wouldn't mind a little more space.

SOLANGE: There's lots of space.

EDDY: Really?

SOLANGE: We don't keep a herd of cattle in here.

EDDY: Just the two of you.

SOLANGE: Yes . . . just two.

EDDY: Hm. You don't find the whole place a bit . . . smallening?

SOLANGE: I don't know.

EDDY: They say close quarters can keep you from expansive think-ing. May account for why Prosper isn't more ambitious, *(indicating sign)* sentiments aside. Think about it.

SOLANGE: Prosper is plenty ambitious. He has plans you don't know about. Still waters run deep, and what seems to stand still may be churning beneath the surface. My husband is a strong current; he is an unexpected undertow. Don't underestimate him.

EDDY: *(amused)* My mistake.

SOLANGE: Any message?

EDDY: Oh, just dropping off a pamphlet for him. And this invoice. He'll know what it's for.

> SOLANGE *snatches the papers from* EDDY *and pointedly cleans up the garden, pulling out weeds from between the stones.* EDDY *takes the hint and leaves.* SOLANGE *picks up the bright stone from the garden, considers, then pockets it and goes to look for* PROSPER.

11. Just That One Thing

SOLANGE enters the bar, to EDIGE's surprise.

SOLANGE: Edige, have you seen my husband?

EDIGE: Not since your beauty first blinded me.

SOLANGE: He was walking in this direction when he left the house. Where else would he go?

EDIGE: A better question: How does he tear himself away from you each morning?

SOLANGE: He can't still be at the lake. Every damn day, listening for long-gone stones to fall. I have followed him. Nothing. All is still yet he sits with his eyes fixed on that spot.

EDIGE: When I close my eyes tonight I'll see you again, standing there in my doorway, but instead of your husband, you will be asking for me.

SOLANGE: Do you think he is hearing something? Does he see her there?

EDIGE: Are you hearing me now, Solange? Do you see me here?

SOLANGE: What? Why do you look at me like that? Please send my husband home if he comes here. Can you do that simple thing for me?

EDIGE: Anything.

SOLANGE: I don't need your "anything." Just that one thing . . . Edige, do you know what this is?

SOLANGE shows EDIGE the bright stone.

EDIGE: A pebble?

SOLANGE: It appeared in my garden this morning and seems to attract snakes. Have you seen others like it?

EDIGE: Not around here, but over the mountain. They are plentiful there. Nothing special.

SOLANGE: Why would anyone keep a stone?

EDIGE pulls a small stone out of his pocket.

EDIGE: Do you remember this?

SOLANGE: What? Remember a pebble?

EDIGE: On the day I first saw you . . . I was walking past your yard when you were coming from a bath. I looked over at you just as a wind lifted up the edge your wrap and a soft thigh peered out and paralyzed me. Still as stone myself. I couldn't move my mouth to give words to this wonder. I watched you bend down and pick up this rock, and you threw it. Really hard. Hit me right here. It was as if you had touched me.

SOLANGE: Okay. Good night.

SOLANGE leaves and goes to the lake.

EDIGE: You went away with a laugh that said, "Wait for me here." And I determined to meet every morning here, on this spot, between your bed and your bath. So that the sight of you going by is like the thought of you coming back. If you would once see me, I could do anything.

> *EDIGE follows SOLANGE. She stops and stands watching PROSPER who is watching EDDY test the water in the lake. EDDY leaves. PROSPER dives into the lake and resurfaces with stones. He sorts through them, keeping the brightest ones and throwing the rest back. He dives once more. SOLANGE leaves; EDIGE leaves. PROSPER brings the rocks home and lays them in the garden.*

12. Flowering

PROSPER and SOLANGE finish eating. SOLANGE clears the table.

SOLANGE: You're still hungry.

PROSPER: No. That was good.

SOLANGE: Drink some water.

PROSPER: Thanks.

SOLANGE: Sorry it's only eel. There wasn't money to buy manioc.

PROSPER: I know. The fish have been small . . .

SOLANGE: I know.

PROSPER: And this eel does not taste good.

SOLANGE: No, it does not. How will I sell it?

PROSPER: Where are my shoes?

SOLANGE: Outside the back door. They were wet, and they smell awful. Did you walk through a swamp?

PROSPER: Mm. That man come by to sharpen knives today?

SOLANGE: No.

PROSPER: Mm.

SOLANGE: Someone came by, though.

PROSPER: Oh. Solange, can you pass me the account book?

SOLANGE: You can practically reach it yourself.

PROSPER: Huh?

SOLANGE: Try.

PROSPER: *(does, can't reach)* Come on. Pass it.

SOLANGE: Try harder.

PROSPER *tries and comes close on teetering on chairtip.*

Don't you find this house a bit . . . smallening?

PROSPER: Smallening?

SOLANGE: Yeah.

PROSPER *tips the chair until he reaches the account book, falls, sits on the floor, and opens it.*

PROSPER: Ah.

SOLANGE: Ah, you see what I mean?

PROSPER: No. What were you saying?

SOLANGE: This house. It's smallening. Limits your ambition. You think?

Pause. PROSPER *looks up.*

PROSPER: Who did you say came by here?

SOLANGE: A man. Didn't leave his name, just these papers. I told him I didn't know where you were. Where were you?

PROSPER: Slick voice, greasy smile?

SOLANGE: Yes. Prosper, I'm asking you—

PROSPER: That is just the limit.

> PROSPER *goes out. He looks in the bar for* EDDY, *who is not there.* PROSPER *goes to the lake and spends the night furiously scooping out algae with his hands. At daybreak he wakes* EDIGE *to begin drinking.*

13. Poets

The bar. EDDY *enters and sees* PROSPER *dozing on a table.* EDIGE *serves him. It is non-negotiable.*

EDIGE: So, is it helping yet?

EDDY: It's definitely moving forward.

EDIGE: Towards?

EDDY: The next thing. That's all progress has to do.

EDIGE: What's next? Say, can I ask you something?

EDDY: Shoot.

EDIGE: Don't you ever want to be . . . useful?

EDDY: I'm plenty useful, brother. I'm a catalyst. A propeller. I bring change.

EDIGE: But why? Who asked you?

EDDY: You don't always know what you need—and you can't always bring yourself to ask for help. Sometimes someone's gotta do it for you.

EDIGE: And that's you.

EDDY: Let's not forget the Fisheries Department.

EDIGE: I've seen you moving quickly, from here to there and back again. What comes of it?

EDDY: Man's gotta move. Life is motion.

EDIGE: You must sometimes wish you could be still. Just suddenly stop what you're doing and stand on the spot where you stopped.

EDDY: For what? So I can hatch an egg?

EDIGE: To understand. To see what's going on, and then to act on that understanding. I dunno . . . just . . . to breathe?

EDDY: I leave that to people like you. The common man. People content to be life's spectators. Look at you. Even while you talk about stillness your hand is working those bottle caps, dying to be doing. Anything. You're bored. You have the potential to be great but you have succumbed to stillness. You don't have what you want, and you're not doing anyone any good, are you?

EDIGE: Depends who you ask.

EDDY: When's the last time you felt alive?

EDIGE: Got hit in the head with a rock once.

EDDY: That explains a lot.

EDIGE: That so? Have another.

EDDY: No thanks. A Coke? I'm not much of a drinker, friend.

EDIGE: Not much of a friend, then. Hmph.

EDIGE leaves him.

PROSPER: Not much!

EDIGE: Ah, shut up, drunky. You know, if that's how you feel, I don't know why you don't just punch this guy in the face.

PROSPER: I would hit him in a heartbeat—if I thought it would bring back the fish . . . or make this glass full again.

EDIGE fills PROSPER's glass again.

EDDY: How long's he been sitting there?

EDIGE: Most of the day.

EDDY: Come on now, Prosper. No reason to be contentious.

PROSPER: Get lost, you . . . freak.

EDDY: Freak?

EDDY laughs in surprise.

PROSPER: Yup. Let me tell you something.

EDDY: Uh huh. Tell me all about it, Prosper.

PROSPER: No! Not telling you nothing. I'm talking to my friend over here.

PROSPER beckons EDIGE.

Barkeep, let me tell you something about this guy. This . . . pffffffft. This guy. Oh boy, I got things to say about him. This guy, he's a piece of work, and I can tell you a thing, a thing or . . . or two . . .

EDIGE: Go on.

PROSPER: This guy is a . . . he's . . . a freak.

EDIGE: So you said.

(to EDDY) Don't let my friend's mood keep you from drinking. He doesn't mean it, I'm sure.

EDDY: It's all right. Matter of opinion, I suppose. They called Magellan a freak, Copernicus, Galileo.

EDIGE: Who all, now?

EDDY: But they were imaginers, like me. People who make things better, for everyone. He says freak, I say poet. Poet-tay-to, poet-tah-to. Ha ha.

EDIGE: Tell us one of your poems.

PROSPER: Yeah, jerk.

EDDY: My poetry is not for telling. It is no mere sound and syllable, but the more enduring medium of cells and cilia.

EDIGE: Was that one? I don't get it.

PROSPER: He's a fiend. Unnatural.

EDDY: Change is hard, Prosper. I understand. When all this is over you and I will laugh together. You will see that progress and innovation are a natural part of our lives. That this science is a thing of beauty.

PROSPER: You don't know beauty. Your eyes are too big to see it. Let me tell you something.

EDIGE: This oughta be good.

EDIGE *tries to fill glasses and is waved away.*

PROSPER: Beauty is the almost inaudible sound of a bright shining pebble hitting the water's surface on the other side of the lake, followed by another and another that says "look over here" in a language few can understand. It is the small ripples spreading out from the source of that sound, and the wider ripples that follow when your lover's lithe body slips through the water's yielding skin. Beauty is watching a woman not watching you watch her bathe, but knowing you are there because she has called you with her tiny ripples. Ah, Ines. If I knew how few were the days left to us, I would gladly have paid double what you asked.

EDIGE: Suddenly I'm drowning in poets and no one wants to drink. Last call, folks.

EDIGE *lays down a handful of bottle caps in front of* PROSPER.

PROSPER: Edige, my good friend, I would not presume upon your generous nature, however I am unable to pay you what I owe you tonight.

EDIGE: How much money do you have?

PROSPER: Exactly zero money.

EDIGE: Did you have the money when you came in and started drinking? Did it go somewhere while you sat here talking?

PROSPER: Ask the freak. No fish, no money.

EDDY once again pays PROSPER's tab. EDIGE addresses EDDY.

EDIGE: I don't know why you don't just punch this guy in the face.

EDDY: Prosper and I know business isn't personal. Right, pal?

PROSPER: Not your pal, you weed.

EDDY: Look, I can see you're passionate about this, so I'm gonna see what I can do. Did you get a chance to look at that stuff I dropped off? I'm offering a special package deal, but it's a limited-time offer.

PROSPER: You can't be serious.

EDDY: I guess you could always go with one of the local eel-supply firms . . . no? Or perhaps you've found another species that thrives in these . . . unique conditions? No again. Then I suppose you'll be leaving your land to find another lake? Taking up another trade? More nos. Well, at least you have something in abundance. Eight o'clock tomorrow, then!

EDDY and PROSPER leave.

EDIGE: Beauty is . . . Beauty is wondering all your life what you were made for, and finally getting a glimmer.

14. Hospitality

Outside the house, morning. PROSPER *is alone as* EDDY
rounds the corner of the house.

PROSPER: This is my little house, which You have built with my own
two hands. There lies that wife of mine whom You love with my
heart, and these are the words You speak with my mouth. This
is the little lemon dove comes to my doorstep each morning, this
same one, and welcomes me to Your day.

EDDY: Who are you speaking to?

PROSPER: To Him who made all.

EDDY: Why are you telling God about your house? Don't you think
He knows already? He watched you build it.

PROSPER: What should I say instead?

EDDY: I don't know. Funny way to pray, though.

PROSPER: And what could I say that He doesn't already know? My
thoughts? My wishes? He knows those, too. Prayer is not God's
news broadcast.

EDDY: Funny.

PROSPER: You're funny. And I don't want you coming around my house anymore. Or my wife. Or my lake.

EDDY: Hey, buddy, let's keep this friendly, huh?

PROSPER: Look, I can't stop you from talking, but go stand in the road while you do it. This is my home.

EDDY moves to stand in the road.

EDDY: All right, all right. I don't hang around where I'm not wanted. But say, friend. Did I mention I have just the thing to fix all your troubles?

PROSPER: I'll bet you do.

EDDY: Yup. Look, I told you, I'm gonna make it all up to you.

PROSPER: Make it up to me? Have you seen that lake? It's covered in green God-knows-what, the fish have all gone, and I can't even imagine anyone wanting to bathe in it anymore.

EDDY: Buddyyyyyy. It's a lake.

PROSPER: This lake is a heart pumping life into limbs of land through miles and miles of river veins. And now, pumping poison.

EDDY: Come on. Forgive and forget.

PROSPER: So much moving forward. Do you ever look behind you?

EDDY: What's done is done. Let's talk about how we move forward from here.

PROSPER: You won't be seeing me, and I'm not your buddy.

EDDY: I'm here. To help. Your wife wants more, Prosper. Won't you try to give it to her?

PROSPER: You don't get to speak for her.

EDDY: I'm only saying what you can see for yourself. Do you ever wonder what she does when you are not at home? What she dreams of doing, given the chance?

PROSPER: Lay off my wife; I'm warning you.

EDDY: Fine. Let me speak in general terms. A woman who is not well kept will keep secrets, and a man who cannot ease her should sleep uneasy. Cheers!

> EDDY *leaves.* PROSPER *goes down to the lake where the algae is worse than ever. Just foaming. He weighs his options and hustles to the bar.*

15. Soul Food

SOLANGE is in the garden looking at the little pile of stones PROSPER has brought from the lake. SOLANGE goes inside and sets the table as PROSPER arrives drunk.

SOLANGE: At least I know you will always be back to eat.

PROSPER: Hello, Solange. You look nice. Let's eat.

SOLANGE: Here you go.

SOLANGE gives him an empty plate.

PROSPER: What's this? Where's my dinner?

SOLANGE: What do you mean? This is your dinner. When I was your wife, I cooked for you and you ate what I cooked. And now that you are leaving me for a ghost, you must begin to eat the food that your new wife will cook. This is your ghost dinner. And I, your pitiful former wife, have nothing to ease my grief. Nothing but this goat bone to gnaw, nothing but sweet marrow to suck between my teeth and roll around my tongue. Your miserable former wife sits alone with her plate heaped to overflowing and no idea how to eat it all, while you fill your belly with a dead woman's love.

PROSPER: Has this table always been so close to the wall?

SOLANGE: You see?

PROSPER: Did you move it?

SOLANGE: Why would I move anything?

PROSPER: I don't know. To make room for all the crazy?

SOLANGE: What's that?

PROSPER: I said maybe to make room for a baby.

SOLANGE: Room? For a baby? Have you never seen one? They take up less space than that broken mower you brought home last month. Prosper, when a baby comes a home makes itself big enough. Let me show you something.

> SOLANGE *goes out back.* PROSPER *empties the wish jar and puts it back.* SOLANGE *returns holding a half-made baby garment, unravelling in her hands, to find* PROSPER *gone. She sees the empty wish jar.*

16. Communing Badly

SOLANGE makes ritual, lays down a handful of seeds, a small branch, and some leaves in a bowl and lights them, then lays the bowl under the bed. At the lake, PROSPER counts the money from the jar.

Long pause.

SOLANGE: Leave us be, you filthy side-striped jackal! Sorry! Sorry. Please. I didn't mean that. I know you were a good girl. Well, at least a clean girl. God knows the whole town has seen you bathing at one time or another, dropping your fat carcass into the water for anyone's husband to see. Sorry! Sorry. Ines. Why couldn't you throw your stones for Edige? Now my wish jar is empty and I know what it costs to bind two souls. I know that when a man spends more time getting less fish something is not right. You have eaten my dreams and taken my reason. Stop throwing your stones into my yard!

PROSPER: One night I will come home and say, Solange my basket is empty. You will bring me into the warmth of your flesh and blood and soothe me with the heat of your mouth. There will be no judgment on your lips and no shame in your eyes.

EDIGE: Leave me be, you majestic crested crane; you unoffered promise; you unredeemable prize. I put myself all around you so that even when you look away I meet your eyes. I put myself at your feet but even when you fall I am beneath you. You have a husband you love and long for, who longs to come home. But no one can fill the gulf between you.

17. Unreliable

The bar. EDIGE *pours a drink that* EDDY *downs dutifully.*

EDIGE: Another?

EDDY: What do you think?

EDIGE: I think you are wearing out your welcome.

EDDY: Resistance to change is only natural. If I know anything about anything I know this: that man can see the only practical option available. Mark my words. Prosper comes barrelling through that door any second . . . Any minute . . . Momentarily. Well it's not an exact science, but he's coming. Pelting down the road towards his last, best chance as we speak . . .

EDIGE: Should I remain on the edge of my seat or shall I pour you another?

EDDY: What the hell. We're celebrating. To progress.

> EDDY *puts money on the counter in imitation of* PROSPER. EDIGE *serves him.* EDDY *slams it back.*

And one more for science.

EDIGE: Whatever you say. It's funny, you don't strike me as the waiting type.

EDDY: He's coming. Another.

EDIGE: Whoa, slow down, cowboy.

EDDY: Not my style.

EDIGE: Who am I to argue. Shall I upgrade you to the good stuff?

EDDY: There's good stuff?

EDIGE: Sure.

EDDY: Line it up.

EDIGE: You got it.

> EDIGE *pours.* EDDY *gulps and spits.*

EDDY: Jesus, it's the same terrible swill!

EDIGE: Well yes, but this one comes in a glass bottle.

> EDDY *checks his watch.*

EDDY: I'm on a deadline here. There's no time for messing around. When he shows up you tell him I waited as long as I could. No, no. You tell him Eddy don't wait for no one. Especially not some fish-stinking pole slinger with crooked writing who's too stupid to find rocks on the other side of the mountain. No wait! Don't tell him that. You tell him when he comes, you tell him, tell him, say I said . . .

EDDY sticks out his tongue, blows a sloppy raspberry, and departs. PROSPER enters.

PROSPER: I came as fast as I could. Where is he?

EDIGE: Left. Pour you one?

PROSPER: Yes. He say anything?

EDIGE sticks out his tongue, blows a sloppy raspberry.

Beat.

Anything else?

Beat.

EDIGE: Nope.

PROSPER drinks and leaves.

18. Love Like a Broken Phone

PROSPER and SOLANGE go to bed together. PROSPER sleeps; SOLANGE watches him.

SOLANGE: What's that sound?

PROSPER: Hm?

SOLANGE: Prosper, I think someone is outside. Will you check?

PROSPER: Mm.

SOLANGE: Prosper. Prosper! . . .

He is sleeping.

I want to climb over this stone in my chest and lay in the valley of your arms.

PROSPER: Mm.

SOLANGE: Prosper. If I reach into the middle of this distance and do not find you there, reaching out too, I will fall and break. Reach for me, Prosper. I would rather be loving than warring.

PROSPER: Mm?

SOLANGE: I said turn over, you're snoring.

PROSPER: Sorry.

He shifts away from her.

19. A Hard Place

Movement Three: SOLANGE *watches as* PROSPER *leaves the house. He sits at the lake, fishing line in the water, but looking at the opposite shore. After a while he returns home.* SOLANGE *watches as he re-enters the house with his empty line. She shakes her head as the buyer passes, lies down, and looks at the wish jar without touching it.* PROSPER *leaves again and she swaddles the jar in cloth, cradling the bundle.*

PROSPER *finds* EDDY *at the lake, which is now slick with algae.* EDDY *is working some pseudo-sciency Rube Goldberg contraption.*

EDDY: Hey! There's my good—

PROSPER: You'll eat the next word.

EDDY: Whoa. Teeth today. Hey, I'm sorry your lake is fishless, but I already told you what I intend to do about it, and I'm a man as good as my word. I am going to get you a whole bunch of the finest eels available. For only a small sum, friend, you can completely restock your lake in no time at all. I have them with me now.

PROSPER: I don't want your eel. I never wanted your eel. I want you to stay away from my lake. I have to figure out how to make the fish come back and get this green stuff gone.

EDDY: Oh, the fish aren't coming back.

PROSPER: What are you talking about?

EDDY: Well, it's an unfortunate side effect we've found with the eel. They change the chemical environment of the lake so that the indigenous species—oh, but what am I boring you for? You're an eel man, now. Pretty soon you'll know more about them than I do, smart guy like you. And that's not to mention a bonus sideline in algae expertise.

PROSPER: I don't want you putting any more eel into this lake. You want me to pay you to put them in, so I can take them back out again? That's not even how fishing works.

EDDY: Move with the times, Prosper. This is how it's done all over.

PROSPER: Really?

EDDY: Oh yeah.

PROSPER: This is the first I've heard of it.

EDDY: You need to get out more.

PROSPER: You say other fishermen are switching to eel?

EDDY: Totally. In droves.

PROSPER: So, if people all over are driving away the fish and bringing in eel, everyone at the market will be selling it, and the price of eel will soon go down until it is even lower than the fish ever was. That's if there is a market for them at all.

EDDY: What? Prosper, don't complicate things. Here's the situation as it stands. You have this lake. Fishie go bye-bye, okay? I have these eel. You have that money. Do you see how this works?

PROSPER: \

EDDY: You're really not a man with a lot of choices.

PROSPER: No. I'm not. Why is that?

EDDY: It is what it is, Prosper. Why is not a question. I'll tell you what. I'll make you a very special deal. Ready? You give me that money, and in return I will give you these eels, and some bait.

PROSPER: These eels are not nearly as large as the first eel you gave me.

EDDY: Nonetheless. The money?

PROSPER: So this is progress.

EDDY: Nice doing business with you.

PROSPER: You've changed everything.

EDDY: Adapt. Human beings adapt remarkably to change.

PROSPER: Adapt! My house is shrinking, my wife is driving me crazy, and now I am giving up a lifetime of fishing to be an eel breeder.

EDDY: Oh, you won't be breeding them.

PROSPER: No, of course not. They'll breed themselves. That's not what I meant.

EDDY: No, they won't. That's what I'm telling you. These eel don't breed.

PROSPER: They just . . . spawn? What?

EDDY: No . . .

PROSPER: The eel fairy delivers them?

EDDY: Close. I'll arrange, shall we say, a monthly delivery? Eels and bait? Of course. What am I saying? Where else would you get it? Anyways, listen, friend. I'm sure you can understand, now that we're going to be doing business so regularly, I can't keep giving you the introductory rate. I gotta make a living too, right?

PROSPER: And we have to live here. What is that smell hanging in the air? What is this sheen on my skin? And the eels frighten children who just want to come down here for a drink of water.

EDDY: Ha ha ha! Oh you're not kidding. No, you don't want to be drinking out of there. Someone should put some signs up.

EDDY *starts to leave.*

PROSPER: Not so fast. Take that thing with you. I don't want any more of your presents. And I'd rather throw myself in the lake than buy a single eel from you.

EDDY: Buddy, I can see you're upset. I'm really trying to make this eel thing work for you, okay? I like you. I really do. Which is why I have already installed a prototype of the Filtrex GS10 depicted in the pamphlet I delivered. Look, I'm not supposed to do this, okay. These aren't really on the market yet, but I figure you're a hard-working guy, someone should give you a leg up. I'm starting to feel like the organization that employs me may have taken unfair advantage of the situation and I'm gonna make it right. There's no need to fear innovation!

PROSPER: Take that thing out of my lake and go.

EDDY: Prosperrrr . . .

PROSPER: Never say my name again.

EDDY: Guyyyy . . .

PROSPER: Not a cent.

EDDY: Oh, that's the best part! You don't give me a penny. This is a demo model, so I can just run it for you and if you like what it does, say no more. If you feel you'd like something more, then we can talk.

PROSPER: If you show up at my house with another invoice—

EDDY: Man of my word, Prosper.

They exit in opposite directions, PROSPER going home.

20. Intruder

SOLANGE is inside the house. PROSPER knocks at the locked door.

SOLANGE: Who's there?

PROSPER: It's me, Solange. I need you.

SOLANGE: Help! Help! Another woman's husband is in my house! He wants to climb into my bed! He wants to kill me and drag me into the yard so that he can bring his new wife into my kitchen and let her use my good red plates! Help me! I am only a widow since my husband certainly died, almost immediately after he left me. Someone help a poor, lonely widow.

PROSPER: I need you to stop this, Solange.

SOLANGE: Would you like me to sit in silence while the two of you exchange mocking whispers and lustful glances? While she eats the food off my plate? Does she happily cradle a spirit child which you have given her?

PROSPER: How should I answer you?

SOLANGE: In some way other than words. Answer me with your eyes. With your hands. Answer me with a basket full of fish.

> SOLANGE *looks out the window to see* PROSPER *destroying his fishing rod.* PROSPER *goes to the lake. He dives in and brings up more stones.*

PROSPER: One day I will come home and say to you, Solange, my basket overflows. You will pour forth your love, rushing in torrents, unimpeded by weariness or disappointment, across this gulf. It will flood the plain and feed into that plot you have tended, giving life to waiting seed.

21. Communing—Mohamed Comes

We see SOLANGE *in her house making ritual.*

SOLANGE *lays down a handful of seeds, a small branch, and some leaves in a bowl and lights them, then lays the bowl under the bed.*

SOLANGE: Ines. Tonight we will talk again, and after this I will never again ask for what is rightfully mine. Let us come to some agreement, you and I, or I will soon join you where you are, and then we will really have a problem.

Truly, I would give you back every stone you have ever thrown if it would rid you of your hold on him and on that place. But I will never again ask you to leave him. I have asked you already what my husband can do for you. You chose not to answer me. Now I ask, what will you do for him? Do you not see him breaking? What good is your love? Help my husband, Ines.

PROSPER *comes home and falls into bed.* SOLANGE *goes to the other side of the lake where* INES *once stood. She has gathered up in her skirt or in a bundle all of the stones* PROSPER *retrieved from the lake. As she passes the bar, she is seen and followed at a distance by* EDIGE. *When* SOLANGE *arrives at the lake she flings the stones into the water, watches the last of the ripples subside, and returns home.*

22. Getting Clear

EDIGE is in the bar. PROSPER enters.

EDIGE: Good fishing today, Prosper?

PROSPER: Are you asking how I'm doing professionally, or if I have any money in my pocket?

EDIGE: Uh huh.

PROSPER: Well to answer both your questions, still no fish, but I do have money.

EDIGE: On the table, please.

PROSPER: Oh come on.

EDIGE: You and I know that business isn't personal, friend.

PROSPER: Don't you start with that friend stuff too.

EDIGE: Sorry. Must be catching.

PROSPER: At least something is.

EDIGE: That guy is a piece of work. I never met a guy the world would miss less.

PROSPER: Tell me about it. But it looks like he may have done at least one thing right.

EDIGE: You don't say.

PROSPER: I'm as surprised as you. One little patch of the lake has started to come back. It's not big but it's definitely blue, and it doesn't have that strange slickness to it—not as much anyways. Calls it the Filtrex GS10.

EDDY enters.

EDDY: Is that my brand I hear?

PROSPER: I was just saying—

EDDY: I know, I know. What you have to keep in mind is these things take time. You have to be patient, because what we're looking for is an incremental recovery. See the demo model is fine, don't get me wrong. It's just, as you're discovering, it may require a small additional investment to yield the kind of . . .

EDIGE: Prosper was just telling me it's starting to work.

EDDY: You have to be patient. Now if you need more immediate results, you want to upgrade from the free model to the Filtrex GS20. I'm not even supposed to *talk* about that model.

PROSPER: No, this one is great.

EDDY: What? How?

PROSPER: What?

EDDY: How nice. What do you mean, exactly?

PROSPER: There's this one patch of the lake that was all green and scummy like the rest of it. This one little patch is already starting to clear.

EDDY: What little patch? Where is it?

PROSPER: On the far side of the lake under—

EDIGE: —under the fig tree.

PROSPER: Yes. Under the fig tree.

EDDY: You say the lake is clearing up.

PROSPER: Yes. The lake is like the skin of a teenage boy just about to enter manhood. Clearing one small piece at a time. Letting us see what it will become.

EDIGE: Under the fig tree.

PROSPER: Yes. Sorry I lost my temper yesterday. I take it back. You can say my name. I am even coming to believe in the beauty of science.

EDDY: Excuse me. I have to go.

EDIGE: Me too. Last call.

23. Love Like a Debt

EDIGE *goes over the mountain in the dark, his receipts clinking. He returns near morning to drop a boulder in the water. He knows it is a drop in the bucket. He is so tired.*

EDDY *exhales a long stream of smoke.*

PROSPER *and* SOLANGE *lie awake in bed.*

SOLANGE: What was that sound?

PROSPER: I didn't notice.

SOLANGE: You wouldn't.

PROSPER: Why not?

SOLANGE: Lot on your mind these days.

PROSPER: Oh. What did it sound like?

SOLANGE: A little like . . . a missed connection. A little like . . . a strong spine groaning under the weight of obligation. A little like a pocket full of bottle caps.

PROSPER: No, I didn't hear anything that sounded like that.

SOLANGE: Go back to sleep.

PROSPER *listens hard.*

24. Blueing

EDDY and PROSPER are at the bar looking over results from the water test.

PROSPER: See? It's exactly like I said, only better.

EDDY: I don't understand.

EDIGE: It's like a miracle.

EDDY: It's something, all right.

EDIGE: It's the next thing, like you said. Progress, right?

EDDY: Yeah. Right.

PROSPER: You sound surprised.

EDDY: Me? No, I'm—It's amazing. That's good. Really good for you. I mean it.

EDIGE: And everybody's happy. A round to celebrate?

EDDY: Shh.

PROSPER: Wow. Look at that.

EDDY: What?

PROSPER: You. You're all deflated. You see this?

EDIGE: Yeah. Are you okay? You look a little green.

EDDY: I'm fine. Just . . . fine.

PROSPER: It wasn't supposed to work, was it?

EDDY: Of course it was . . . a little bit, but it was never supposed to do all this. It's never done this before. Something's gone very wrong.

PROSPER: Something like you accidentally fixed the lake before you could upgrade me to the Filtrex GS20? Can you hear yourself? You're upset because your product has failed to fail. Your product, which doesn't usually work, worked. And you say that something is wrong. Doesn't that seem wrong to you? Something is right for the first time, and for the first time that mud-sucking grin has been wiped off your face.

EDDY: This just . . . changes things.

PROSPER: Oh yeah? How so?

EDDY: Just hold on a minute.

EDIGE: Why, you hatching an egg?

PROSPER: My friend, a piece of free advice? Adapt. Human beings adapt remarkably to change. Next town you're in, maybe you can hang around an extra day instead of scurrying away like a roach before a broom.

EDIGE: Like a fly from a swatter.

PROSPER: Like a fish from a hook.

EDIGE: Like a rat / from a sinking ship.

EDDY: Shut up. How am I gonna explain this?

PROSPER: How about explaining this instead: Why is it you're afraid of selling a real product, one that works? What would you be like if you actually believed in what you were doing? I mean you could go back to all those other lakes you screwed up and do them some good.

EDIGE: People might not want to punch you in the face anymore.

EDDY leaves.

PROSPER: I'd better go clean my rod.

PROSPER leaves. SOLANGE enters.

EDIGE: Solange.

SOLANGE: Have you seen my husband?

EDIGE: Every word you say to me doubles my strength as my heart grows inside my chest, pumping hope through wasted sinews.

SOLANGE: Did he say where he went?

EDIGE: Prosper has gone to clean his fishing rod.

SOLANGE: His fishing rod . . . You look tired. Have you been sleeping?

EDIGE: Only in hopes it will bring this very vision.

SOLANGE leaves.

And when you finally look at me and see me in front of you, I am as good as ten men, each differently dedicated to your heart's desire.

25. Love Like a Lowered Shield

PROSPER goes down to the lake, tastes the ungreening water. SOLANGE appears on the far shore under the fig tree. She throws a stone into the water. He sees her.

PROSPER: What are you doing here?

SOLANGE: I wanted to bathe.

PROSPER: Here? But everyone will see you.

SOLANGE: I thought that was part of it.

PROSPER: Part of? . . .

SOLANGE begins to disrobe slowly while speaking.

SOLANGE: Our life together has become too small for you. Prosper, I don't know what has happened to us, but I would do anything to unhappen it.

PROSPER: You don't understand.

SOLANGE: I don't. Where are my wishes?

PROSPER: Solange, I am trying. I am trying so hard right now— Put that back on. People might come.

SOLANGE: Prosper, I am trying. I am trying so hard right now.

PROSPER: That's enough.

SOLANGE: Answer me, husband.

PROSPER: I spent them. Tomorrow the truck will come with bricks, and I will build another room on our house.

SOLANGE: Bricks. After all . . . Is this what you offer me, husband, in place of flesh and blood? Do you really think some stones can save us?

PROSPER: Wait—

PROSPER hurries to cover her before she can be naked and embraces her from behind.

Here is your answer, wife. See? How my chest is shaped to cradle your spine? How my arm is curved to bring my hand round to your breast? How my neck is bent to inhale your sweet sweat . . .

SOLANGE: Yes?

PROSPER: Come, let me show you what those bricks are for.

He gathers her up and takes her home to bed. Let's not watch this part.

26. Love Like a Drop

PROSPER and SOLANGE lie awake in bed. EDIGE *comes back over the mountain in the dark, grunting under the load of an impossible boulder that he drops into the water, which echoes the sound of real stones dropping.* EDIGE *makes a second trip across the mountain, returning with another stone. His image multiplies, echoes into a line of ten gitaga drummers, each with a stone/drum on his head.*

PROSPER: What is that sound?

SOLANGE: I didn't hear it.

PROSPER: You wouldn't.

SOLANGE: Why not?

PROSPER: Heavy sleeper.

SOLANGE: Oh. What did it sound like?

PROSPER: A little like . . . a dream coming to an unexpected end. A little like . . . love surfacing to breathe. A little like a stone dropping into the water.

SOLANGE: No. I didn't hear anything that sounded like that.

PROSPER: Go back to sleep.

SOLANGE listens hard.

27. Epilogue—Beauty Is

SOLANGE communes. PROSPER *is at the lake with a rod in the water and the empty wish jar beside him.* EDIGE *stands at the mountain's base with a small bag/suitcase.* EDDY *is elsewhere, giving a Filtrex demo to a crowd.*

SOLANGE: Ines. Can you hear me? Have you gone? The lake . . . the lake is nearly blue again. Prosper has told me that the fish will return after some time. It will be hard until then but . . . he whispered it to me last night across that vast space between our pillows where you once lay. I think that you are really gone. I don't know who I will blame now when I burn the corn. This is peace between us, Ines.

PROSPER: Little one, did you see your mother smile when she said goodbye this morning? It was a smile of welcome. Welcome to our lake, where I will teach you to fish. Those high grasses over there will soon become a roof for the little room we are building. That sad little school swimming there will become plentiful. Through faith, perseverance, and the labour of our hands will we prosper. And maybe even through the beauty of science, a little bit.

EDIGE: Solange, today you came to me as I have always hoped you would. Today you looked into my eyes and said my name and all weight lifted from my twisted spine. Your eyes were clear and your voice full when you said to me, "My husband is fishing." Your hand gently cradled the air where a belly might one day grow and your happiness broke the blindness that love once lay on me. This is the happiness I toiled for. Yours. This is it.

He feels unwell.

I hope that it is good to you.

EDIGE *leaves town.*

EDDY: Ladies and gentlemen, neighbours, friends! I know my previous visit did not turn out quite as we all had hoped, but risk is a close companion to innovation. I tell you, I have seen the miraculous results with my own two eyes. Would I be here if I didn't believe in the product? You have to expect a little delay of course. I mean it's science, not magic. Now if you'll just bear with me, I can assure you that the Filtrex GS10 is everything I described. Not sure why it's not . . . You're good, hard-working people, so I'm not gonna try to put one over on you. Now hold on, I know I said you'd see a difference by now but this is for real. Wait, step back now. You don't want to do anything rash. Say, have I told you about the Filtrex GS20? Wait, wait . . .

EDDY is frantically adjusting the apparatus while the light shrinks to a pinpoint on his face.

Acknowledgements

AMAF was developed in residence at the 2011 Stratford Festival Playwrights' Retreat, and in Toronto with support from Obsidian Theatre and actors Cole Alvis, Omar Hady, Jivesh Parasram, and Leah-Simone Bowen. The play received a public reading as part of the 2012 Prismatic Arts Festival in Halifax with actors Cole Alvis, Jivesh Parasram, Tara Lee Reddick, and Jacob Sampson under the direction of Leah-Simone Bowen. Indispensable encouragement was provided by Yvette Nolan, Shuni Tsou, Sanjay Shahani, Blake Sproule, and Hugh Neilson. Thank you to Mary Wong for the inspiration of her painting, *Out of the Blue.*

Donna-Michelle St. Bernard is an emcee, playwright, and administrator. Other works for the stage include *Gas Girls*, *Salome's Clothes*, and *Cake*. DM has been playwright-in-residence at Obsidian Theatre, Dynamo Theatre, and Canada's National Arts Centre; general manager of Native Earth Performing Arts; co-editor with Yvette Nolan of *Refractions: Solo*; lead vocalist for Belladonna & the Awakening; and artistic director of New Harlem Productions.

First edition: October 20.
Printed and bound in Canada by Imprimerie Gauvin, Gatineau

The cover art is a deatil of the diptych *Out of the Blue* by Mary Wong,
www.marywong.ca.
Author photo © Denise Grant

**PLAYWRIGHTS
CANADA PRESS**

202-269 Richmond Street West
Toronto, ON
M5V 1X1

416.703.0013
info@playwrightscanada.com
playwrightscanada.com
@playcanpress

A **bundled** eBook edition is available
with the purchase of this print book.

CLEARLY PRINT YOUR NAME ABOVE IN UPPER CASE

Instructions to claim your eBook edition:
1. Download the BitLit app for Android or iOS
2. Write your name in **UPPER CASE** above
3. Use the BitLit app to submit a photo
4. Download your eBook to any device

MIX
Paper from
responsible sources
FSC
www.fsc.org   FSC® C100212